To

Tessa, Elise & Brooks

From

The Strattons

For my dear little nieces,
Eleanor and Annabel   A.W.

Written and compiled by Sophie Piper
Illustrations copyright © 2015 Antonia Woodward
This edition copyright © 2015 Lion Hudson

The right of Antonia Woodward to be identified as
the illustrator of this work has been asserted by her in
accordance with the Copyright, Designs and Patents
Act 1988.

Published by Lion Children's Books
an imprint of

Lion Hudson plc

Wilkinson House, Jordan Hill Road,
Oxford OX2 8DR, England
www.lionhudson.com/lionchildrens

ISBN 978 0 7459 6554 3

First edition 2015

Acknowledgments

All unattributed prayers are by Sophie Piper and Lois
Rock, copyright © Lion Hudson.

p. 8: Sarah Betts Rhodes (1824–1904)

p. 12: W. St Hill Bourne (1846–1929)

p. 18: From an old New England sampler

p. 21: Author unknown

p. 24: Traditional

p. 28: Walter J. Mathams (1851–1931)

Bible extracts are taken or adapted from the Good
News Bible © 1994 published by the Bible Societies/
HarperCollins Publishers Ltd UK, Good News
Bible© American Bible Society 1966, 1971, 1976,
1992. Used with permission.

A catalogue record for this book is available from the
British Library

Printed and bound in China, March 2015, LH25

Bible Promises for
Baby's Baptism

Written and compiled by Sophie Piper
Illustrated by Antonia Woodward

LION
CHILDREN'S

God made you, Little One

Dear God,
It was you who brought me safely through birth,
and when I was a baby, you kept me safe.

Psalm 22:9

6

Bless my hair and bless my toes
Bless my ears and bless my nose
Bless my eyes and bless each hand
Bless the feet on which I stand
Bless my elbows, bless each knee:
God bless every part of me.

God loves you, Little One

"God loves you, so don't let anything
worry you or frighten you."

Daniel 10:18

God, who made the earth,
The air, the sky, the sea,
Who gave the light its birth,
Careth for me.

God will always help you

"Do not be afraid," says God. "I am with you!
I will make you strong and help you."

Isaiah 41:10

Who made the sun?
Who made the day?
Who made the hours
for work and play?
God made them all,
God made them good,
God helps us live
the way we should.

11

God will hold you close

I will put my trust in the Lord; then I will be content and at peace, like a child lying quietly in its mother's arms.

From Psalm 131

Help us to remember
All your love and care,
Trust in you and love you,
Always, everywhere.

A children's hymn

13

God will turn tears to laughter

O God,
You have changed my sadness into a joyful dance.

Psalm 30:11

14

Praise God on the noisy drum
Rumpty tumpty tumpty tum.
Praise God with a mighty clash
Let the cymbals crash-a-bash.
Praise God on the gentle flute
Tootle tootle tootle toot.
Praise God as you pluck the strings
Tring a ling a ling a ling.
Play the trumpet, rum pah pah
May your praises sound afar.

From Psalm 150

God will bless what you do

We know that in all things God works
for good with those who love him.

Romans 8:28

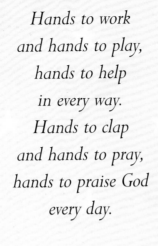

Hands to work
and hands to play,
hands to help
in every way.
Hands to clap
and hands to pray,
hands to praise God
every day.

17

God will bless those you love

The world and everything in it belong to God;
the earth and all who live on it are his.

Psalm 24:1

God bless all those that I love;
God bless all those that love me;
God bless all those that love
those that I love,
And all those that love those
that love me.

Traditional

18

19

God will take care of the world

God promises this: "As long as the world exists, there will be a time for planting and a time for harvest. There will always be cold and heat, summer and winter, day and night."

Genesis 8:22

20

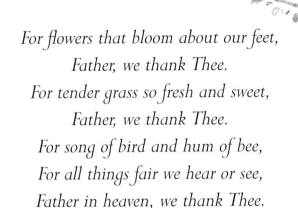

For flowers that bloom about our feet,
Father, we thank Thee.
For tender grass so fresh and sweet,
Father, we thank Thee.
For song of bird and hum of bee,
For all things fair we hear or see,
Father in heaven, we thank Thee.

21

God will show you the way

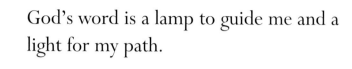

God's word is a lamp to guide me and a light for my path.

Psalm 119:105

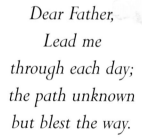

Dear Father,
Lead me
through each day;
the path unknown
but blest the way.

God will watch over you this night

When I lie down, I go to sleep in peace;
you alone, O Lord, keep me perfectly safe.

Psalm 4:8

Now I lay me down to sleep,
I pray thee, Lord, thy child to keep;
Thy love to guard me through the night
And wake me in the morning light.

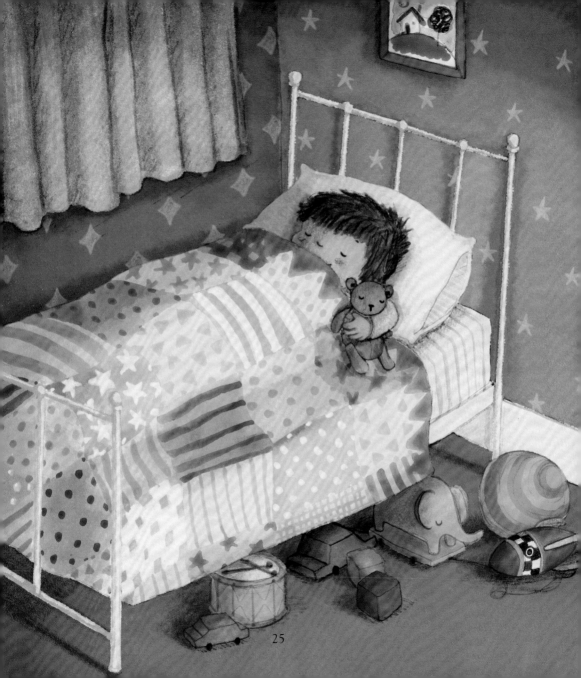

25

God will be your shepherd, little lamb

God says this: "I will look for those that are lost and bring back those that wander off... I am to my people like a good shepherd to his sheep."

From Ezekiel 34:16

Dear God, you are my shepherd,
You give me all I need,
You take me where the grass grows green
And I can safely feed.
You take me where the water
Is calm and cool and clear;
And there I rest and know I'm safe
For you are always near.

Based on Psalm 23

God will be with you for evermore

The Lord will protect you from all danger;
he will keep you safe.
He will protect you as you come and go
now and for ever.

Psalm 121:7–8

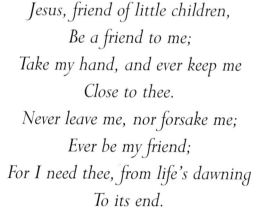

Jesus, friend of little children,
Be a friend to me;
Take my hand, and ever keep me
Close to thee.
Never leave me, nor forsake me;
Ever be my friend;
For I need thee, from life's dawning
To its end.

A children's hymn

28

*May God bless you and take
care of you.
May God be kind to you and do
good things for you.
May God look on you with love
and give you peace.*

From Numbers 6